There is a Ticking in my Head

Xin Yi Zheng

BookLeaf Publishing

Presentation by *BookLeaf Publishing*

Web: www.bookleafpub.com

E-mail: info@bookleafpub.com

ISBN: 9789357445016

First edition 2022

DEDICATION

To my parents, and their personal triumphs. My mom, for her determination to read all my works by herself. My dad, for seeing how happy this makes me.

To Jun Yi - for your friendship and support.

To all the individuals who make me feel less lonely, one day at a time.

To you, reader, for giving my work a chance.

ACKNOWLEDGEMENT

Recognition to the artist of my charming avatar, the Plant-Mom Sun Bear, is due. It was designed and drawn by Cindy, whom I first met through this collaboration. Please find below her details if you would like to see more of similar artwork.

Name/ Tag: Y L WONG(Cindy)
Instagram: @yinlw_space

Short Bio: Hi! I'm Cindy Wong, a freelance illustrator based in Hong Kong. I love to do line drawings with lots of pen strokes(especially with fountain pen) and digital illustrations with strong colour contrast . This is my first time drawing an avatar for others, thanks for giving me this chance!

The poems may be boring for many, and even trivial. All pain experienced is mental and emotional.

For this small collection, I did so daily for two weeks up until the submission deadline. I have recycled no old poems, and am unlikely to present the poems you read here anywhere else.

PREFACE

Thank you for reading the thoughts I am unable
to say out loud and for giving me parcels of your
time. I hope you find what you are looking for.

I do not have what it takes (The Introduction Poem)

I know.
I do not have what it takes,
But spilling out helps, and it soothes the burns
it calms my storms,
it mutes the clap of thunder and skin

because claps echo up here in the mind,
Things do not live past twenty
under the watchful unforgiving eye of
my own disgust.

and I awake each day just to think:
again and again,

"So this is what it takes."

whilst I give and give, unspooling,
the thread of my attention slowly
winding around and around,
undisciplined

to the cities on the surface of leaves,
and the sizzle of butter and egg white,
to souls nailed to the necks of benches,
and rows and rows of averted eyes.

I walk silently, constantly fretting inside
murderous, and afraid of my murder
because here is the killing blow
to all that I am -
the catch-22, broken glass in my ribs
"I know, I know, I know"
    alone, I sigh to me

because it really is just me up here.

I do not have what it takes.

Counting it out (The List Poem)

Where do I begin?
Count them with me

Near empty libraries.

The sound of typing.

The   in conversation, spilling air.
   dips
  The voice of strangers, spearing me.

My mother's laughter.
  The spark of her ecstasy. It burns a war onto
the canvas of my skin.
Let me tell you how,
Hellfire is nectar.

Dogs: those happy, heavy, flopping creatures.

Polishing the cuticles of my fingernails.

Soft rose shores bordering vanilla yellow skin.
The shine of youth giving way to white decay,
dead and stronger.
   I clip them,
   and think of blood.

My father's approval.
   He stands, barely on the edge of video calls,
   looking back at the blob of my identity, my
mess, how I cry.
   He stands, resolute in his past
   tender expectation the flavour of soft custard.

People. I'm pretty certain of this one, I think.
   No. Yes. No. Yes. No. Yes. No. Yes. No. Yes.
No. Yes. No. Yes. No. Yes.

Supported soles, and a well-supported soul. For
this,
a pair of good leather shoes
some bandaid
a bit of tear and blister
the tune of a whistling flute.

I have a song
and it goes like this:
   a dime a dozen, a time to doze,
a lime a lemon, a wasted rose.

The Cowherd (The Valentines Poem)

The sun rises, an overripe yolk
Hilltops a sensual purple horizon.
Above, the magpies are a circling horde
As if ready to alight from nature.

Have you heard of the cowherd
who waits eternity in exchange for
a touch of the weaver's hands?
The very same,
Roughened by splinters and threads.

He likes to trace the terrain of her smile,
the dimples in her cheeks
like the tops of steaming yam buns
and place his lips against her forehead
which tastes like peaches,
a reminder that Heaven is distant.

Liver-spots of age seem to pass
from his hands to hers.

His eyes grow more tired by the second,

Starlight forming bulbs of burden on
the clay of his skin
the brick in his lungs
the mud that coat his feet,
He stinks of mortality, pressed against her.

A foolhardy Tithonus - who is young,
Glistening, athletic, and wonderful.
He is nothing here without her
gaze, a lingering searchlight.

Light! They board an arch of monochrome
wings,
only bags of air,
that puff and screech
Complaining of cold.

Then all too quickly,
she begins to fade,
Her eyes become frantic, catching
the whimper that escapes his lips.

The magpies scattering with relief,
Returning to dirt and dust
Casting their minds to the little ones,
The malleable they who press themselves
onto blankets of wildflowers.

They, who will need to eat soon

and sleep
and have their faces washed
and hummed to
and kissed
under the heave of a deep violet night,
elbows and knees plump
lives dipped in rosebud.

The cowherd has forgotten
How hope feels like in the way
his heart aches and cries.
That silent anger coursing through his veins
as he alights too, irked
a lack of poetry in his movements,
proof of Heaven's impatience.

The din in his ears
grows louder and louder,
His pride a thinning coat
stitched by his turning resignation.

So he keeps jealously close,
The warmth in her hands
one thorn in the sides of eternity
as the evening bells bring him home.

Something about the smog (The Homesick Poem)

Something about the smog
from home
That clouds the mind's judgment.

I sip a cup of Oolong tea
Wishing I had more to say
about the place that cradled me

Yet here I wait
For the recognition of foreigners
as trauma glares back
The screens I keep bright
gardening shears for my loneliness
trimming the baby hairs of nostalgia.

I push a mouthful of noodles in,
perversely waiting
for a rush of memory but find nothing.

Something about the smog

from home
It starves the soul, tempts, and twists.

I cry for home - the perfect picture of surprise
all the while clawing at a false future
Full of things
I cannot hope to possess.

Something about the smog,
from home
Like the air in a taxi ride
Or the impossible green parks
And the miniature imposter bakery
tacked onto the side of Chinatown
It has lost me
just as I feel I am slowing down
unravelling rapidly each evening
becoming bitter and still.

And still,
I long for the anti-cotton heat,
an awkward undefined nationality,
A citizen inheriting a culture
Held together by mutual frustration.

I call to the smog,
I sing along to its song.
Something about it, something about it.

A day with Delaroche (The Art Poem)

I cannot know her
Silk cascading over bent knees,
neck cocked.

She is stretching herself forwards,
reduced to blindness
bound in hand and eye.

Held close,
the prayers are whispered
her arms prickle at the touch of strangers.

The emerald velvet holding her
bends under her weight,
The executioner resists a sigh.

So I sit here and wait indefinitely too
I have all day,
to imagine the bloody sequence.

Watching her is a comfort,
as I promise myself,
that I might die with her.

Yet she is suspended above me,
in time
and in frame
bathed in pearl and light and gold.

She won't die,
not here
where my eyes
do not wish to close.

Your eyes water
(The Tube Poem)

Conversations rising to
slap
against the roof of the train car
ringing disharmony in the Central line

I look straight ahead of me
at the words of another, glued to the roof
I drink it in -
The pleasant melancholy keeps me company.

It speaks of autumn,
and of loneliness,
presenting in cupped palms
the fluttering heart of a dying robin.

Beside me a stranger sifted through
London's exhalations
sidles into the crook leftover in stale humidity.
I keep my eyes straight ahead of me
Lips thinned in steady neutrality.

I wonder if others are afraid too, as I

furtively dart from man to man,
their foreign blue-green eyes seeming to water
under the grimy tube lights.

Acid, river, virus, feet.
Underneath the cover of water and moss
shooting through the belly of this city,
All that my mind musters turns to filth.

A tickling in my nose,
The train pauses and jerks forward two steps
Depositing strangers the way a dog gags,
Lungs full of water.

Conversations grow longer and longer,
Their beat and rhythm refusing to work together
To the panicked circling of flies dragged in
With the stench and sweat and skin of us-
we watery creatures,
forever unsatisfied - because
Tomorrow, we return again.

Me, Jungle Asian
(The Alien Poem)

Hello,
I say. It is polite, delicate, in order
to minimise the dimming
at the corners of your wrinkled smile
dips over the lily-bleach of your gaze
and how I feel, an animal in the zoo.

Hello,
you reply, maybe. I wouldn't have heard
I'm sorry ma'am,
I was too busy worrying about
whether you
with cheddar palms and wine-laced breath
have already made your decision.

Before you,
the warm tea of my pleading irises
reduce themselves to mud.

Nervously, I am
Not fancy, or Japanese or doing well -
I was not taught to whisper and be

skirmish. I do not giggle naturally.
The territory of battle is not the same
mark the caution in my voice.

Me, Jungle Asian from the equator
touched by the sun and shielded from the ugly
in the hopes that I would not turn out ugly.

I know what you are thinking.

I think those things too, sometimes.

The lacquer at home is not a national treasure,
the V&A Museum has no need to document it,
It's just gong-gong's old cupboard
and it is as dead as he is.
I crouch there still, with my hands on my knees
a second and a half pair of breasts ballooning
if I tucked my thighs under my t-shirt.

Did you know, ma'am,
I used to fold handkerchiefs into the shape of
panties
And shriek in a playground with my friends.

Somehow you're still here,
I don't have time to unpack everything
but if I may just squirm a little more,
grabbing you by the collar with my teeth

I hold you in place
I say,

Hello, I am here
All the while worrying that others,
those much better
Have already ensnared your focus first.

I am a whimpering dog
Bad at healing, shocked by wetness
Tonight I will go home
Fry an egg and soak it in cili sos,
hating the ochre undertones of my skin
so desperately scrubbed away by ginseng pills
My mother took daily in pregnancy
so that I would be devoid of history
and of the canvas of my roots.
I wish I could gently coax myself out,
and show you

Rainforests flooded with natural remedies,
excrement and death,
Wide-eyed and clumsy
I have no accent that is my own.

Cast a thought to the world's stinkiest flower
Me, Jungle Asian
though I have never lived in a jungle,

but among stainless steel cutlery and automated
car doors
breathing nothing but the same air
fearing the same pathetic discomforts.
Before you I keep standing
and pretend that I am any different.

How do you do, I continue,
You're still here
but there is a muscle prick
you look behind me,
That must be the invisible monster.

I cannot see him but everyone else seems to
It looms over me and shows you things
Should I tilt my head and obstruct you?
The way protest obstructs protest,
in this strange big spiderweb sky-glass city.

When I finally turn away and release you,
my mind will likely reel with a little jealousy.
With your high and full laughter
echoing cream and crystal halls,
always both fully aware and half-asleep.

Later, when you think yourself safe,
I might even catch your eye
as a waitress serving you dessert.

I tried to love a boy
(The Love Poem)

Wasted time
Plans decayed and fell,
It lasted as long as a calendar sheet
Ripped down from its holster by hand.
I crawl under my bed sheets every night
Fists clenched for luck.

Maybe you won't visit me tonight
To trample and scream at me
In the form of a sneering shadow
I keep you in my dreams
Purely out of spite.

One of us looked the other way
And I could see the clock hands move
It is a curious thing, to like someone
To actively reject him as he looks at me
Arms open, heart closed, mind empty.
You make me feel small and helpless,
more than I already do.

Before me the river continues to flow

You are every duck and mention of Devon.
If I turn around all I will see is transport
And you will occupy my mind like tape.

This is the product of my cruelty
It rushes at me in ambush
Years and years of self-infliction
The way I was touched
The way you did not leave room for me
to breathe
I had already lost you before I loved.

And when I finally catch up to you, just by
a finger's width, skin stretched taut over
grinding herbivorous teeth,
You dropped the anchor tied to my foot
Sinking me, and left me to seethe alone.

So I tried to love a boy, but
It didn't end when he said it had.
Even in my departure he gives no comfort.
Instead here it is still, curled up and content
to make a dark home behind my eyes.

So I tried to love a boy, a laugh
for a liar like me, liar
I cry at my reflection,
and crave sleep,
and tire.

Where I put all this fear (for my breaking)

When writing anything purposefully
Every sentence should be a gift,
wrapped so tightly in knots that it chokes,
struggling for air.

Every sentence I can write is angry
frustrated, indignant, misplaced
and here I remain, sitting in my chair.
What is this fidgeting I do?

I have committed no crimes in
crushing the spice of shame
self-inflicted and odourless as carbon monoxide
preparing hope under mortar and pestle
a bitter concoction that hugs me back.

In accordance to some unknown design,
I lay out the tools in a row before me.
With repetition, so follows memory -
The double-edged sword to my fractured ego.

Weaker and weaker still,
each time I host my own imprisonment
Playing the role of judge, warden and
executioner
before sunrise, and long after sundown.

It is the horror stories and coffee stains
the way I wistfully build a version of myself
through
a collection of others' just rewards,
a tapestry of girls with white teeth.

A sociopath - and not even a good one at that.
Here is something that made a girl laugh once
I said to her, in a doctor's waiting room, I said -
"I hate my body, it is shaped like a carton of
milk."

But this is not a comedy,
and perhaps you have already stopped
chasing after my misery,
it becomes all and much the same story.

What is this poem? Where does it go?
It is a child borne only from the slipperiest parts
of me
The catfish, the cunning fox.

Most dislikable, opposing weight to my
happiness.
I have put some here
and still shake from caffeine,
eyelids heavy with the night and
the full inventory of my regrets.

I remind myself,
wilfully ignoring the way summer makes
sticky faces and itchy necks
in the sauna of my room, my veins.
Dragging this current me that I love -
gagged with her hands bound, and
month-old tears staining her cheeks

Look here, girl, I say to her -
Every sentence should be a gift
Beautiful and elegant and desirable.
You better lock the door,
and love yourself a little more
as you wish upon your wishing stars
the kind of death that keeps you alive.

What a mess you are
the fruit of a diseased mind and slow hands.
What a mess, this is bound to leave a scar.
Rip this page out - throw it away.

It was not as if she did nothing (a poem-about-another-poem)

Fleur Adcock,
from Auckland, New Zealand,
spoke to me in a museum bookshop.
Because it was not as if I did nothing
Prowling the intestines of the Linbury Galleries
A social orphan,
eagerly looking for escape.

The page landed gently,
as if the spine was roused from a nap
and my gaze, walnut shaped and awkward
Made a beeline to the inner world
of a Miss Hamilton.

Oh?
Hamilton's portrait, Lady
Hamilton the founding father, Sir
but this is another Hamilton entirely.

I do not know her,
and yet within the first two lines,
I knew her better.

This other woman, young and adult both -
visited bookstores
and carried her errands at her elbows
Mushrooms, black pepper, and rent
counting out the routes of
her youth, her time
only noticeable to strangers if she spoke
if at all, so little noticeable
Already asking quite a lot.

I let out a breath of relief,
Amazed to find my lonesomeness
staring back at me.
She is alone, I thought,
Inhaling museums as I stand in a museum
and inhale her.

I pick up a little vase between thoughts,
as Miss Hamilton picks up her skirts
and settles herself into her seat at the table,
Up here - where I have laid out
Afternoon tea for both of us.

I gather my hairs
(The Dust Poem)

On the other side of the window,
Two large bees collide into the glass
Thwacking at the sides of my head
They reel away in shock, unsteady.

My fingers poised, palms spread to
Sweep semicircles on the floor
Eyes darting towards the insects,
Flitting back to my mess.

My fallen hairs, bundles of dark hay
Fishing lines for dirt and grey lint
Form crop circles on the infertile soil
Raising conspiracy before my eyes.

Quickly, with disgust,
I pinch my hair between my fingers
Alongside silverfish that occasion the curtains,
We scuttle for the plastic jaws of the bin.

Teacup in my hands
(for lunch)

Looking out across Soho
Where two grizzled women sit
Legs crossed and puffing.

Their fingers cinch a cigarette each
As time had cinched the lines around their eyes
Overfed crows waddling around,
Steps trailed by crow's feet.

I am indoors, with a friend,
Who sits and considers the menu
as I consider my day.

She lifts her head when I lean over
Asking her what she wants.
In my hands I cradle my tea cup,
Hand-painted and dark blue
It is my pet,
Keeping me still and calm.

Pickled vegetables
A side of roasted meat,

Or is it the other way around?

Next to us, sitting close
Three young women like us,
Hold a negotiation as their knees
try not to touch.

What am I afraid of, I wonder
So much so that this tea cup
Holds me in place?

My friend offers a follow-up
Her response chasing the silence
Pointing to the noodles on shells
to my nodding along.

If I bend my neck back (for nightmares)

When I go to sleep,
My neck is crooked,
Head cocked to listen like a gun.
Sometimes I look into the mirror
Somebody else grins back at me.

Yet there may be another horror
The one that has made its bed
Deep at the back of your mind
Lodged, inflamed, a scarlet red.

When you take a shower
When holding a common kitchen blade
When the train comes thundering along
Or a kettle masking the sound,
of a crime ready-made.

All this is silly,
And rhymes to make a merry tune,
Up through the alleyways in your brain
Looping along to an owl's croon.

When you roll under your sheets,
Snuggled, warm and ready for sleep
There may be a shadow
Waiting to puncture, flesh-deep.

How much of it, I wonder,
Can each of you take
Before there is breakage
Splintering, blistering,
Your brain - an organ - baked.

To serve, cooled, on a tray
Separated into eight equal parts
Enjoyed with some cream and butter
Salted to taste,
Now next, is the heart.

I shall give you rest
(for the rested)

I shall give you rest,
Restoration and slumber
We will moult out of our milky old skin.

I will hold your wish,
By a red-gold string
And place my hands together for hope.

I will feed you still,
Every year under the sun,
Laying out a feast to dine with you.

I promise you assurance,
Keeping my tongue still
If you choose to visit in all your forms.

I shall give you rest,
Praying for your good health
In the hope that you watch over mine.

You will pass me by,
In new voice and face,
One day when cycles begin again.

If tomorrow you change (for witches)

At the bank of a cold river
You hover at its edge, pensive.

Nails bitten, lips cracked
The soles of your feet numbed.

The village where you are is waking up,
A masculine sun looming distantly.

There are spells that can fix this,
Charms and potions that may help.

But you bite your cheek,
Fixing your eyes instead on the dark basin.

There are horrors worse than hell,
An empty threat spat by empty people.

Your wrists itch with the screams of others,
Sunk under pebbles with callous shine.

You consider how they will chant your death,

Execution of a villainy that lives only in them,

If tomorrow you change,
It is not the form of a human you will take.

Further and further the river calls,
Dark arms outstretched in blue.

Something clutches your elbow and keeps
Your resolve locked in your bent ankles.

There is a moment when you contemplate
How the hens in their coops will need feeding.

Still, you hesitate, the shadows sneer
Still, you stop.

If tomorrow you change,
There will be more that meets the eye.

Eye-level the sun shifts upwards an inch,
You turn to look back at the cottage roofs.

If tomorrow you change,
What will you do now?

Raising ghosts after dinner (for some friends)

I cut into the lamb,
Squeezing out the conversation and red.

Around me,
We chase the laughter
As if children could be afraid of stumbling.
We open gifts,
We discard past gripes,
Our claws are dulled under romantic ambient
light.

There is a promise hanging in the air
Comfortable night runs to the supermarket,
perhaps
We are too brightly lit
Flushed red from our shoulders.

When we settle deeper
In somebody else's home,
Nursing our mugs of alcohol.

I run my gaze almost lovingly over
the blush of your cheeks
the outfit you carefully picked out
I skip, internally, from one state to another.
You could be anyone
Yet here I am, firmly in place
Laid out on a reclining cushioned seat
And admitting to you my depths.

I fall back instead on the safety
Of being among companions,
Reminded of these irrational fears.

We speak of ghosts
And shriek at our own youthful foolishness.

Around me,
Air rife with ripples
We will cry another time.

Just before I am pushed back into the night
I am surrounded by the warmth of farewells.

Under my skin it sits (to my anger)

I watch from behind the gaps
Acid rising to my soured tongue
this collective learned dismissiveness
Tilts me further into turbulence.

In my room is where I settle
Moulding thoughts in slowed time
feeling pathetic and small and ashamed
Quickly to the fire I run.

There's the River Lea from my window,
And the roads where rage whistles and stomps.

Today I made children tremble
But it is the children I blame
the sirens blaring in my head
As my mother commands me to mantra.

From my dinner to slumber
Slumped and closer to lifeless
Admitting that the more I despise
The more fearful death becomes.

Goldfish and love letters (for the younger me)

Look around you, soak it in.
It will not last.
Choking,
You play the waiting game

At the back of your father's car,
In the dark cocoon of your room
Under the glare of your smartphone.

Something shimmers in the water
And time is ticking on. Breathlessly,
Your head bobs up with apple-flush

I lost pieces of you,
Drifting atop the rubber squeak of escalators
Rosebud lights
And the clinking of glass.
Those scars you carved
Pushed into a pile of wishing bones.

Your world is one of air-conditioning
Of carefree ease and cheese fries
Worrying about your width and span.

Yet you crave to hurt. Scraping
All manner of things, from your knees
to your heart.

So write about goldfish fireworks
Glitter stuck in your fingerprints
Red packets and love letters

I cannot promise
My constant support for you.
Yet,
being bound is also a comfort.